Have you ever thought about how...
Complex problems bring you to your knees.

35

PRAYER: Holy Father, hallowed be thy name. Look upon me now, on bended knee, bowed in heart and body. Waken my ears to listen like one being taught. Open my soul to your power, O Sovereign Lord. Set my face like flint to do Thy will. I want to receive Your love and grace. Fill me with Thy presence that I may walk in the light of your fire. Speak to me Lord. Your word is my solution. In your light there is life. Through the Lord Jesus Christ, Amen.

Have you ever thought about how...
Complex solutions bring you to your knees.

Begin with...

GOD, IT DOESN'T MATTER HOW I PRAY, OR WHAT WORDS I USE. MY PRAYER IS IN MY INTEN-TION: LET ME BE WHO I NEED TO BE.

SHOW ME HOW TO DEAL WITH BUZZ, AND THEN LIVE LIKE WHAT I BELIEVE.

HELP ME, DEAR LORD, TO DEAL WITH IT.

AMEN.

But God's answers aren't so simple either.

Maybe it would be easier if God just handed out a list. You know, with sins and consequences clearly marked out—like "The Top Three Ways to Deal With It." Like, 1) Just don't smoke pot or you'll get a plague of grasshoppers in your house. 2) Don't ever drink alcohol; if you do, your car won't start. 3) If your friends offer you stuff, get all "Nehemiah" on them—punch them, kick them, etc. (see Nehemiah 13: 25 for specifics).

But he tends to give us stories instead.

37

Stories that show shame...

Thoughts on being BUZZed from
NOAH'S HUNGOVER BRAIN
(taken from **GENESIS 9:20**)

Uh, let me think here. Uh, God told me very clearly that He was going to destroy all mankind BECAUSE OF THIS PROBLEM CALLED SIN. Uh, yeah. SIN. I knew that.

And, uh, then God told me to build an ark because He was going to send a flood BECAUSE OF SIN. Right. Right. Right. I remember that.

Then waters flooded the earth for a hundred and fifty days, and me and my family were on this ark, and no one else was, BECAUSE OF SIN. Oh yeah, that whole SIN thing—right, that rings a bell.

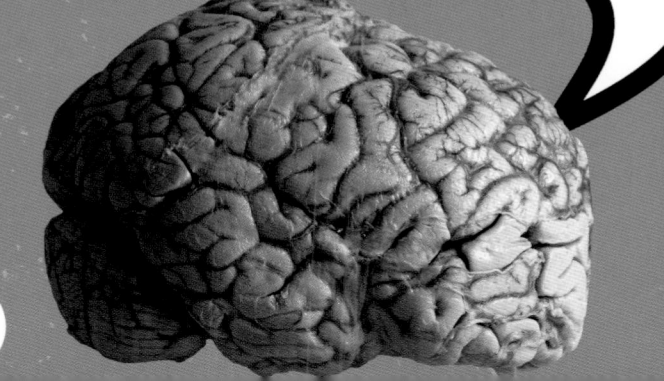

38

Then the ark finally got to dry ground and we all got out, and God gave us a rainbow in the sky as a sign that He was serious about never destroying the earth again BECAUSE OF SIN. And we all agreed to that because we all knew by then that SIN was a bad, bad thing.

And then after all that stuff I know happened BECAUSE OF SIN, the very first thing I did when I got off the ark was this: I planted a vineyard, grew some grapes, made some wine, got drunk, took off all my clothes, and laid around. Then my son saw me naked. So I cursed him and his descendents forever. I wonder, was that SIN, or WHAT?

WHAT WAS I THINKING?

Stories that show really wrong decisions ...

NOT IF HE WAS THE LAST GUY ON EARTH

A lesson on being BUZZed from Lot's two daughters
(taken from **GENESIS 19:30–38**. . .really)

So, there are these two sisters, right, and you won't believe what they do. Their whole city has been destroyed—I mean, like War of the Worlds, Armageddon, whatever. It's bad. And, granted, they're pretty freaked—it's just them and their dad left on the entire planet, basically. But you know how we always say "Not if he was the last guy on earth"? Well, they figure their dad is the last guy on earth, and if they're ever gonna have kids, he's the only chance they've got. So they make a plan to get him drunk and sleep with him. Yeah, I said they want to sleep with their dad. And they do. Seriously. How messed up is that?

40

KING "I CAN DRINK BOOZE FOR A WEEK" XERXES
(from **ESTHER 1: 1–20**)

KING XERXES: *Hoo boy, what a hangover. I can't believe I was drunk for a week. But whoa, what a party! You should have seen everybody—on the floor, the chandeliers. Man, were we baked. Oooh, if only I could remember what happened.*

MEMUCAN (KING'S LOYAL SERVANT): *Uh, hate to tell you this, King, but when you were drunk you attempted to publicly humiliate your wife by having her parade around in front of you so all your drunk cronies could check out her hot bod.*

KING XERXES: *Oh. I did that? Well, what happened?*

MEMUCAN: *She politely declined, your majesty.*

KING XERXES: (long pause) *Hmmmm, so what happened then? I'd like to see her soon.*

MEMUCAN: *You signed an irrevocable royal degree saying that she could never ever be in your sight again. She's completely banished from your presence for the rest of her life.*

KING XERXES. (longer pause) *Really? Are you sure? I really liked her.*

MEMUCAN: *Really.*

KING XERXES: *Rats. So, uh, what do I do now for a wife?*

MEMUCAN: *Well. Why not have a huge beauty contest where you line up all the virgins in the country—thousands of them. Have a great big contest where you sleep with each one for a night, then they go into your harem, probably never to be seen again (their fathers, brothers, and boyfriends surely won't mind). When the contest is over, you can pick the one you liked the most and make her your new queen.*

KING XERXES: *You know, Memucan, every once in a while you come up with a peach of an idea. Round up the virgins!*

42

Why Solomon could never write ad copy for a wine company...

Don't judge wine by its label,
or its bouquet, or its full-bodied flavor.
Judge it rather by the hangover it leaves you with—
The splitting headache, the queasy stomach.
Do you really prefer seeing double,
with your speech all slurred,
Reeling and seasick,
drunk as a sailor?
"They hit me," you say, "but it didn't hurt;
They beat on me, but I didn't feel a thing.
When I'm sober enough to manage it,
Bring me another drink!"

PROVERBS 23: 29–35 *(THE MESSAGE)*

VIN ROUGE · PRODUCT OF FRANCE

Solomon's Vineyard

REELING & SEASICK

12% alc/vol. · 950 B.C. · 750 ml

IT'S YOUR LIFE.
YOU MUST
DEAL WITH THE
CONSEQUENCES—
WHATEVER
DECISIONS YOU
MAKE.

DECISION # 1: To follow the law or not.

In the United States, it is illegal to buy or possess alcohol if you are under 21. Some states allow exceptions for religious or medical purposes or on private property. For most provinces in Canada, the legal drinking age is 19. In the United Kingdom, it's 18, unless you're in a restaurant, where the age limit is 16.

Pot is illegal throughout North America, but there are exceptions in Alaska and some Canadian provinces, and for medical use. It's your responsibility to know the law in your area.

Possession and use of every other drug, such as cocaine, Meth, LSD, magic mushrooms, etc., are illegal.

45

Consider all the fun things that can happen when you don't follow the law:

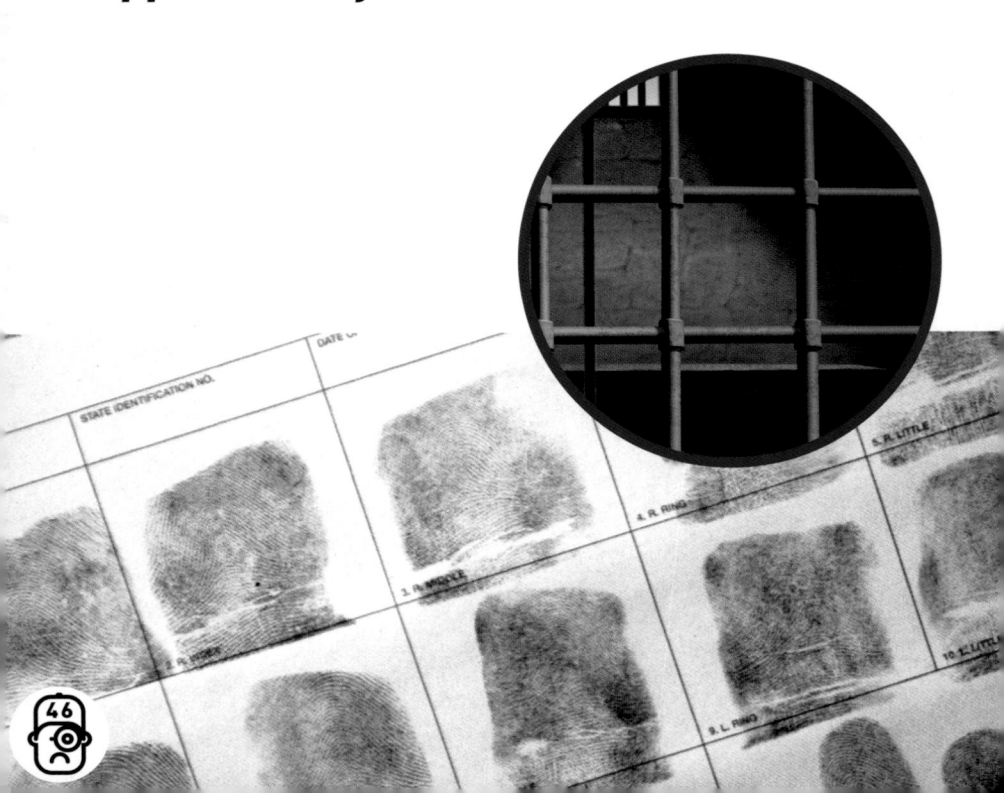

GETTING ARRESTED, GETTING HUMILIATED IN FRONT OF YOUR FRIENDS, *GETTING PATTED DOWN,* GETTING A RIDE IN THE BACK OF A COP CAR, *GETTING FINGERPRINTED,* GETTING STRIP-SEARCHED, *SPENDING A NIGHT IN JAIL,* SEEING A JUDGE, *HAVING YOUR PARENTS PAY FINES,* YOU PAYING FINES, *LOSING YOUR DRIVER'S LICENSE,* PICKING UP TRASH BY THE SIDE OF A ROAD, *SPENDING TIME IN JV LOCKUP,* GETTING KICKED OUT OF SCHOOL, *HAVING A CRIMINAL RECORD FOR THE REST OF YOUR LIFE,* HAVING PROBLEMS GETTING INTO A COLLEGE OR TRADE SCHOOL, *NOT BEING ABLE TO VOTE,* HAVING PROBLEMS GETTING A JOB, *HAVING YOUR CAREER CHOICES LIMITED (E.G., MUCH HARDER TO WORK WITH CHILDREN,* BECOME A LAWYER OR MEDIC, *TO WORK OVERSEAS, ETC.),* HAVING PROBLEMS GETTING INSURANCE OR *A LOAN FOR A HOUSE*

WHAT DOES THE BIBLE SAY ABOUT OBEYING THE LAW?

Everyone must submit himself to the governing authorities, for there is no authority except that which God has established.... Consequently, he who rebels against the authority is rebelling against what God has instituted, and those who do so will bring judgment on themselves. Submit to the authorities, not only because of possible punishment but also because

DECISION # 2: To be logical or not.

It seems simple: Drugs are harmful, so don't do them.
But drugs are cool. And you want to be cool.
So maybe it's not so simple.

What if something else harmful for you was cool?
Would you do that too?

GIRL 1: Hey—what's with all the guys at this party? None of them seem to like me.

GIRL 2: They've all been castrated. It's cool.

GUY 1: Do you think that girl over there is hot?

GUY 2: No.

GUY 1. Me neither—high five! Man, there's nothing like getting your tads lopped off. It sure is cool.

GUY 2: Yeah, but not only your tads—you should lop off your jimmy too. I did.

GUY 1: You're right. That's even cooler. Hand me a knife, will ya.

DECISION # 3: To find a safer BUZZ or not.

WHAT'S THAT MEAN?

There are a lot of well-meaning people out there who believe the answer to BUZZ is trying to minimize the risks of alcohol and drugs. That's what the whole idea of having a designated driver (or "Key Master") is all about. You still get BUZZed, you just get home safely that way. Another idea receiving a lot of press right now is a drinking party that your parents provide for you in their home—you still get high, you just do it with adult supervision.

The concept of providing a safer BUZZ is like the principle of handing out condoms at school. You're going to do it anyway, aren't you—so at least be safe about it.

50

DOES THAT WORK OR NOT?

It's your decision.

True Story

Rhode Island parents Bill and Pat Anderson recently threw an after-prom party at their home for their son, Gregg. Their idea was that their son and his friends were going to party anyway—may as well do it at home where it's safer.

About 50 kids showed up at the party. At 3 a.m., the police showed up, responding to a noise complaint. The officers took names and addresses, and drove away with the kegs.

One week later the officers showed up again. This time they arrested Bill Anderson, the father. Reason: It's illegal for adults to provide alcohol to minors.

SOMETHING ELSE TO THINK ABOUT.

Even at the "safest" chaperoned parties, what that usually means is that mom and her boyfriend are upstairs watching TV. They're certainly not down in the family room keeping an eye on who drinks what.

And now for the fourth & most important decision . . .

DECISION #4: To do something better with your life or not.

It's your choice to screw up your opportunities. It's also your choice to do something better with your life. What would your life be like if you consistently chose the latter?

A story is told about a man trapped in a New York City elevator during the events of 9/11. Knowing he would probably not make it out of the World Trade Center alive, he took out a small notebook from his briefcase and wrote the following:

If anybody finds this, know that I never gave up. I never took the easy road. I never did what others pressured me to do if I believed differently. I have lived the richest, fullest life imaginable, and I regret nothing.

To my wife, I love you more than anything.

To my children, do wonderful things with your life...

DO WONDERFUL THINGS WITH YOUR LIFE.

With Your Life

I play rugby in fall. In spring I run track, mostly so I can stay in shape for rugby season. I used to drink a beer or two with my friends every once in a while, but I found that the day after I drank I always ran a bit slower. I just don't want to do that to my body. Sports are more important to me.

Chris, age 17

My Mom's an alcoholic. I've seen how much she's messed up our family. I'm never going to touch the stuff. Someday I'm going to own my own card shop.

Emma, age 16

I think the most important advice I can give young people is to have an independent mind. Take the time out to learn about who you are and what you believe in. Individuality is a necessity to becoming a wise, intelligent, and creative person. In the end, follow your gut instinct, and always remember that every decision, good or bad, has a consequence.

Jose, no age given

The night Susanna broke up with me, I went over to my friend Jeremy's apartment and we played cards and drank a six pack. He had two, and I had four. The next morning I woke up and felt horrible. Take it from me, whatever pain you have the night before, drinking doesn't make it any better. The pain is still there the morning after.

Bryan, age 18

I want to graduate from high school and attend an arts college. And I will not have a "job"—I will have a "career" so that I can enjoy life to its fullest. I plan to have a career as a novelist, poet, and an actress. I also want be a plus-size model for Sean John...I think that'll be hot!!! Why don't I do drugs? Once upon a time I promised myself I wouldn't sway any way the wind blows.

Shacoya, no age given

Hi I am fourteen years old, and I started smoking pot when I was eleven. I hung out with a group of guys much older so I could get weed whenever I wanted. I thought I could trust them. I was wrong. One night after my thirteenth birthday I snuck out and went to this guy's house. I got pretty high. It started to get really late, so I decided to leave. He didn't like that. He kept begging me to stay and telling me he'd give me a ride home later. I knew I'd get caught if I didn't leave. As I got up to go he turned out the light so I couldn't see a thing. Then he pushed me back onto his bed and raped me. That night I learned a very crucial lesson: "A friend with weed is a friend you don't need."

Snow, age 14

I'm nineteen, and I've never drunk alcohol or used drugs. I figure I've made it this far, so I'm never going to. I just imagine telling my grandchildren that I've never drank or used drugs.

Spencer, age 19

I started smoking weed when I was in seventh grade. Worst decision I ever made. Why, you ask? Let me just tell you that I am now nineteen years old, and I never graduated high school. In fact, all the education that I have for myself is a GED that I am not proud of. I mean, I had goals for myself. I also read that teens that do drugs are more common to become sexually active than those who don't. Well, I believe that, because I did become sexually active at a very young age and now have a ten-month-old daughter. As you all can see, yeah, drugs may seem to be the cool thing to be involved with, but trust me when I say that *"DRUGS WILL ONLY MAKE YOUR LIFE HARDER!!!!!!"* So just think about what's really important—the party scene? Or your future?

Nikki, age 19

hi there im ethan and i am in rehab, i've been in it 4 like 1 year now, i was addicted 2 weed and coke. it messed up my life and it will mess up yours if u choose drugs, i am getting through it with help from friends and family, i was 12 when i made the stupid decision 2 take drugs, i am now 17, i did it 4 like 5 years, but now i am in rehab and getting over my addiction. dont take or use drugs u dont need them, they completly reck your life and your mind.

Ethan, age 17

58

I went to camp for a week this summer where I rededicated my life to God. The day I came back, my friend, Ava, called me up and we went over to her house where we shared a bottle of vodka. When my dad found out he was really mad. I was disappointed in myself too. I don't care what Ava says, I'm not going to do that anymore.

Fallon, age 14

Doing drugs costs too much. I'd rather play videogames.

The Lone Moon, no age given

What would I say to a friend who is experimenting with or using drugs? I would inform them that drugs will kill your spirit, your body, and mind. I would encourage them to get help, and I would be there every step of the way to help them through a very difficult time. I would attend meetings with them and visit them in rehab. When people have problems, they need prayer and good friends to encourage them to try to better themselves. What they don't need is someone to put them down.

Da Von, age 15

60

DEAL WITH THIS...

Therefore do not be foolish, but understand what the Lord's will is.
Do not get drunk on wine, which leads to debauchery.
Instead be filled with the Spirit.

EPHESIANS 5:17–18

Being filled with the Spirit is not a drug. It is not a rush, a high, or a BUZZ.
But it means being under an influence that is not your own.
Being filled with the Spirit will not cause you to fall down in a water-filled ditch.
You will not get date raped when you are filled with the Spirit.
You will not get hung over, baked, fried, stoned, or smashed.
You will not puke on your shoes.
With the Spirit, the old order of things has passed away.
You have a clarity you never imagined.
When you are filled with the Spirit, nothing is the same anymore.
You have a love that speaks the truth.
An elation that opens doors.
A stillness that clears a brawl.
You swim up waterfalls.
You stage dive with angels.
You are who you were meant to truly be.

MAY GOD GRANT YOU COURAGE,
WISDOM, AND THE FILLING OF THE
SPIRIT AS YOU DEAL WITH IT.
AMEN.

FLIP SWITCH

www.flipswitch.com

We have an antidrug campaign come to our school every semester. All the leadership and student council kids get involved. They have a big assembly with a lot of music, and a speaker comes in to give us a talk. I guess it's effective, but I still know a lot of my friends get stoned every weekend. Why is that?

Jason, age 13

Is alcohol that bad, or is it more of a neutral thing? I don't think alcohol is despicable. I think it's more what people do with alcohol that's despicable.

Marty, age 17

When questions are this tough to answer, there's really only One Person to ask.

FLIP
HERE

More Questions . . .

What I just don't get is when your parents tell you to not drink, but then they always have a bunch of booze in the house, drink wine at every meal, and serve drinks with every party they have. If it's okay for them, why isn't it okay for you? Sure, it's legal for them, and it's not for us, but what I don't get is a drug is still a drug—isn't it?

Juan, age 15

In my high school there's this back door near the gym with an overhang that everybody calls "the smoke pit." It's where all the druggies hang out at lunch and between classes. People sort of look down on them, but the thing is, it's also kinda cool to hang out there. That's what I don't get. People at school act like drugs aren't cool, but then again, they also act like they are cool. So which is it?

Mira, age 14

Seems like the surefire solutions aren't so surefire. Seems like there are more questions than answers.

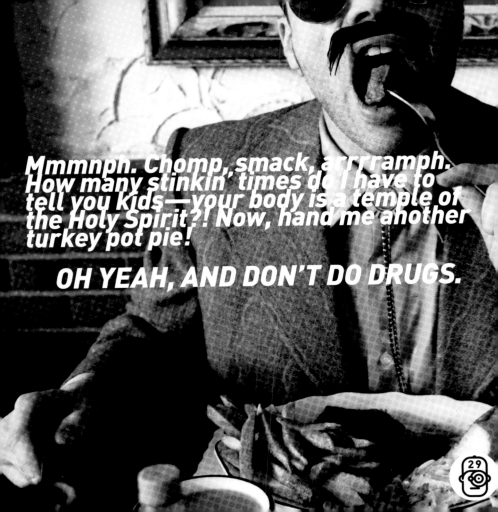

QUESTION: IS THIS, OR IS THIS NOT, A SUREFIRE SOLUTION?

"DON'T DO DRUGS, KIDS, BECAUSE YOUR BODY IS A TEMPLE OF THE HOLY SPIRIT!"

Our pastor always tells us we shouldn't smoke, do drugs, or drink because your body is a temple of the Holy Spirit. He always quotes some teacher of his at the Bible college he went to that used to say: "Your body wasn't meant to be a chimney or a distillery"—which I think is kinda funny. But, if all that's true, then why don't all Christians I know treat their bodies with more respect? I mean, plenty of people in my church are really out of shape.

Morgan, age 17

This is what I love about Jesus. Jesus is all about gettin' high. That's right, (cough, cough). I buy Jesus from some skanky dude on NE 234th Avenue. I just slip the dude two Hamiltons through a hole in his door, and I get a little baggie with enough Jesus in it to last me all afternoon. I cook up a teaspoon of Jesus, wrap my arm with a rubber belt, find a vein that's still got some blood in it, and jab that Jesus right into my body. Whoa, Jesus just starts pushing through me—a million volts of Jesus. That's right, man, I just love Jesus. I can't live without Jesus. Jesus is my high—he's the best drug around.

I just became a Christian, but I don't know if I'd say that Jesus is my high. It's like you're reducing Jesus to some sort of alternative drug or something. Is that what following Jesus is all about?

Steve, age 17

QUESTION: IS THIS, OR IS THIS NOT, A SUREFIRE SOLUTION?

"I DON'T GET BUZZED ON DRUGS OR ALCOHOL BECAUSE JESUS IS MY HIGH."

26

'Ere dude, (huh huh)... just say no to this... (huh huh huh)

You can know something is wrong, and even say you won't use it. But when you're at a party and someone hands you something, it's a lot harder to say no. What are you supposed to do then?

Isabella, age 19

QUESTION: IS THIS, OR IS THIS NOT, A SUREFIRE SOLUTION?

"JUST SAY NO!"

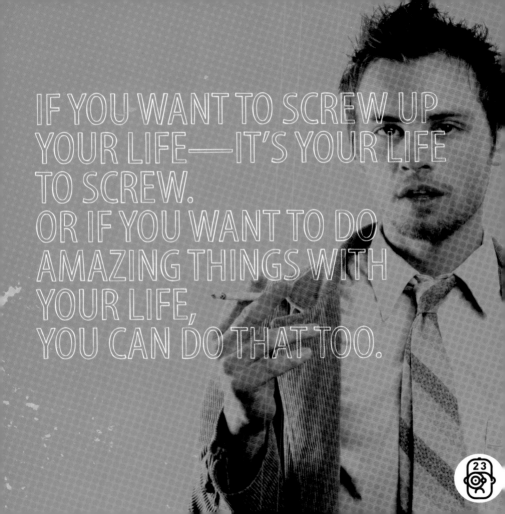

No matter what: The BUZZ screws you. Ecstasy fries your brain's ability to think and store memories. GHB, a sedative that can immobilize you, is frequently used in "date rape" and other assaults. Meth causes mind and mood changes such as paranoia, delusional thinking, long-term depression, and permanent psychological damage. Inhalants make you lose your sense of smell, experience nausea and nosebleeds, and develop liver, lung, and kidney problems. Pot can lead to anxiety, panic attacks, depression, and paranoia. Steroids can cause acne, huge mood swings, depression, irregular menstrual cycles and infertility in girls, and reduced sperm count and testicular shrinkage in guys. Cocaine interferes with the way your brain processes chemicals that create feelings of pleasure, so you need more and more of the drug just to feel normal. People who become addicted to cocaine start to lose interest in other areas of their life. Heroin is highly addictive, and destroys brain function and any ambition other than for getting more heroin. Alcohol is perhaps the worst of all drugs because it is almost universally socially approved and even encouraged. It impairs judgment, inflames passions, and invites violence. It is the common link in car accidents, teen pregnancy, child abuse, divorce, fighting, theft, rape, and all-around stupidity. It does the most harm to the most people worldwide.

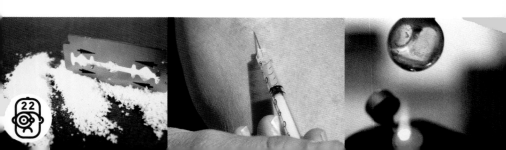

You know it. When asked to choose your favorite TV commercial in a recent study of teenagers, television, and alcohol ads, more of you chose Budweiser than any other brand, including Pepsi, Nike, and Levis. This past year you saw more television ads for beer than for gum, skin-care products, cookies and crackers, chips, nuts, popcorn and pretzels, sneakers, noncarbonated soft drinks, and jeans.

Advertisers dig you—they especially dig young chicks. Over the past year you saw more alcohol advertising in magazines than adults did, and if you're underage and female, you were more exposed to this advertising than underage guys.

The BUZZ is here. Almost one in five of you drank in the last thirty days. About one in ten of you say you are binge drinkers, about one in forty-five of you call yourself a heavy drinker. The older you get, the more likely it is you'll drink more. If you're twelve years old, only about one in forty-five of you drink regularly. If you're twenty-one, more than one in three of you drink regularly.

The BUZZ is at your school. One in four seniors says they currently smoke pot. One in five freshmen do.

And guess what. If you smoke pot, you are four times more likely to become pregnant or get someone pregnant than another teen who has never smoked pot. If you're sexually active, more than a third of you say that alcohol or drug use has influenced a decision to do something sexual.

The *BUZZ* is here.

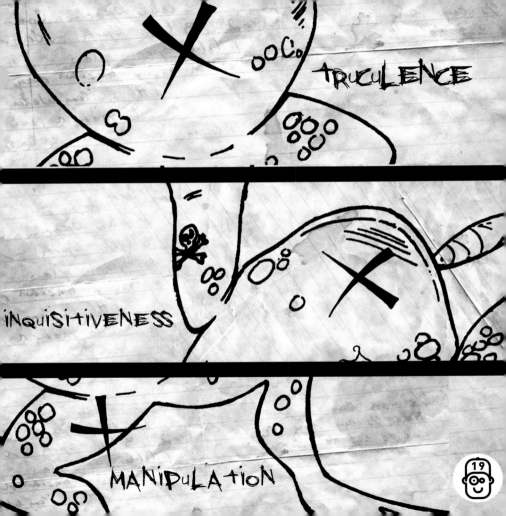

Looks like we've got him all figured out.

TRUCULENCE means that there's this natural defiance that comes with being young—a type of automatic desire to do dangerous things. Sometimes it's not you being truculent, but those around you: Either way, you can't escape dealing with the concept of truculence.

INQUISITIVENESS means you deal with the natural desire to wonder about your world and try things out. Everything is new at your age, and asking "What's it like?" (whether or not you actually participate in something) is part of what makes you, you.

MANIPULATION means you deal with the fact that all around you friends, enemies, and advertisers are pushing you to do stuff—some of it is healthy stuff, but some of it is really dangerous.

But you already knew all that stuff, didn't you?

TOP SECRET

TOP 5 RULES FOR ADVERTISING EXECUTIVES
(Or, how to get rich selling legal drugs to teenagers)

1. Whatever you're selling, your aim is to make teenage consumers absolutely desire it. They must crave your product. They MUST want it. And they MUST want it now!

2. If what you're selling is in any way harmful to teenagers, you'll produce commercials that actually warn them about your product. They'll still want what you're selling. (In fact, they'll probably want it more.)

3. You never actually "sell" the product. You "sell" what the product does for the teenagers. It's how it can make them feel. It's who they'll become. They'll become the sexiest girl. The hottest guy. The person who doesn't have any of a regular teenager's problems.

4. Produce the absolute best commercials money can buy. People should tune in to the Super Bowl just to watch your commercial—not stupid old football.

5. The measure of success is getting the teenager's money. You have no other goal.

L·281

TOP 5 LINES
FOR YOUR FRIENDS TO GET YOU TO DO WHATEVER THEY WANT:

1. EVERYBODY'S DOING IT.
2. WHAT ARE YOU, SCARED OR SOMETHING?
3. DO THIS, AND I'LL BE YOUR BEST FRIEND.
4. DON'T DO THIS, AND WE'RE THROUGH.
5. C'MON, JUST ONCE.

VARIATIONS EXIST, BUT ONCE THEY LEARN THE BASICS, ALL THE POWER IS THEIRS

How's it going? You're looking good today. Been working out? Lost weight? New shirt? There's something I've been meaning to talk to you about. Let me roll down my window. Nothing to be scared of. This is just between you and me. Check this out. Up there, through the leaves. Everyone's eating them. All the cool people, that is. Not interested? Don't chicken out. It's all good. What's the matter, anyway? Did your mama tell you that you couldn't? Would she really stop you from doing something that would help you? Everybody's doing it. You don't want to feel left out, do you? Here, hold it in your hand. It looks good doesn't it.

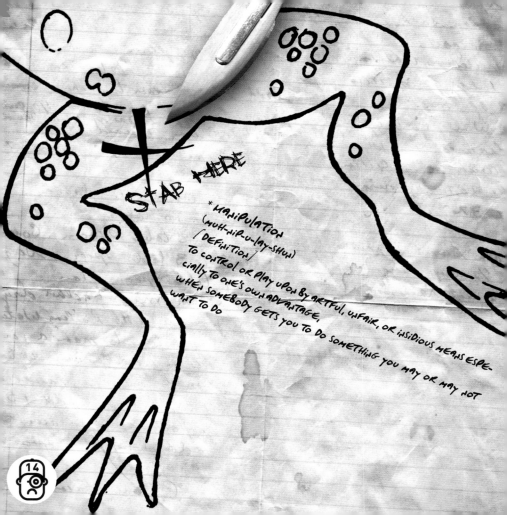

STAB HERE

* MANIPULATION
(muh-nip-u-lay-shun)
[DEFINITION]
to control or play upon by artful, unfair, or insidious means especially to one's own advantage, when somebody gets you to do something you may or may not want to do

DEAL WITH IT

What's it like to get a **BUZZ?** A little **BUZZed?** Even absolutely **BUZZed?** I mean like **BUZZed** off your butt? What will I see? What will I feel? What does it taste like? What does it smell like? How does it feel when you hold it in your lungs? Will I get high the first time? What if I eat a big meal first? Will I get **ADDICTED?** Will I feel relaxed, even silly? Or sexy, grown-up, cool? Will I lose my balance? Will I still be able to drive? What will I remember afterward? Will I get paranoid? Will I get the munchies? Where will I get it? Who will I do it with? Is everybody doing this? Who will find out? What will my friends think? What if I **PUKE?** What if I pass out? What if I stand on a table and make a fool out of myself? Can I still be on the swim team? How long will it stay in my system? Will this keep me out of college? Will I be "in" on some sort of inside joke? Is this legal? Will I get **ARRESTED?** Will I want to do harder stuff? Will I need to steal stuff to get my fix? Will my body be damaged? Will I get liver disease? HIV? Will I die? Will **JESUS FORGIVE ME?** What's it like? What's it like? What's it like? What's it like?

DEAL WITH IT

Okay, now count up yer yeses. How'd you do?

0–2 Yeses: *What a stinkin' Sunday-pants Goody Two-shoes you are. Go back to your mama and cuddle your teddy bear.*

3–5 Yeses: *Still a loser. In fact, you're the biggest loser ever because you just think you're cool. Truth is, your nothin' but a flat-footed dork-weed with snot for brains.*

6–8 Yeses: *Marginally cool. Which is nothing, really. So you're actually still a Gatorade-drinking, candy-cigarette-eatin', nine-cents-short-of-a-dime dork.*

9–10 Yeses: *Congratulations, jerk. You're really really cool. But only you. And me.*

HANK HASBEEN, the Maverick Renegade Troublemaker, who graduated sixteen years ago and still hangs out at your high school, presents:

The "How To Be Absolutely Stone-Cold Cool" Quiz

Listen up pencilnecks. Are you cool? I mean, really really cool? To see if you are or not, take the following quiz. Grab a pen and answer yes or no:

1. Yes/ No   *I get drunk every Thursday, Friday, and Saturday night.*
2. Yes/ No   *I lie about how much alcohol I use.*
3. Yes/ No   *Beer is necessary to have fun.*
4. Yes/ No   *I have frequent hangovers.*
5. Yes/ No   *I smoked pot today.*
6. Yes/ No   *I frequently forget what I did while drinking.*
7. Yes/ No   *Last Thursday while drunk I slapped a cop.*
8. Yes/ No   *I sleep in my own vomit.*
9. Yes/ No   *I give booze to my cat.*
10. Yes/No   *I've had fake ID since I was 13.*

DEAL WITH IT

LIES. LIES. LIES. LIES. LIES.

Five absolute lies: **ONE.** When you get a BUZZ, it won't make you cooler. Lie! Truth is, getting a BUZZ makes you the duke of cool. **TWO.** When you get a BUZZ, you won't have a good time. Lie! Truth is, with a BUZZ, you're dancing on top of the table. **THREE.** When you get a BUZZ, it won't dull your pain. Lie! Truth is, getting a BUZZ makes you forget all the hurt you're going through. **FOUR.** Big companies are socially conscious and don't want you to get a BUZZ at your age. Lie! What are all those funsy, outdoor, extreme-action commercials all about? What are all those candy-flavored vodkas with cool people at parties all about? The earlier you start to get a BUZZ, the sooner you'll be a life-long customer, spending money on their stuff. So drink up, smoke up, shoot up, snort up—as early as you can, nothing makes us happier, man. **FIVE.** When you get BUZZed, and later repent of it, you won't have a great testimony. Lie! You'll have a great testimony. Everybody knows you need to really wallow in sin first before you get your life right with God. With a couple of really good BUZZ stories under your belt, you'll hold 'em captive 'round the old summer-camp fireside. You'll be the absolute poster child for getting your life squared away with Christ.

LIES. LIES. LIES. LIES. LIES.

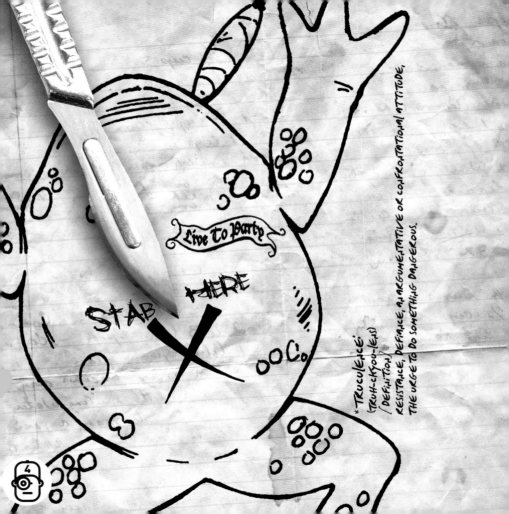

There's this really ugly problem with no easy answer. It just won't go away. So what are you going to do about it?

There ain't one easy answer

for a problem that hits you from a million different directions. This is something you really have to think about, really dig into, really grab a scalpel and dissect, so that you can find the answer that works.

Where do you start?

You start with that ugly amphibian that stares you in the face every day.

And you stab the frog.

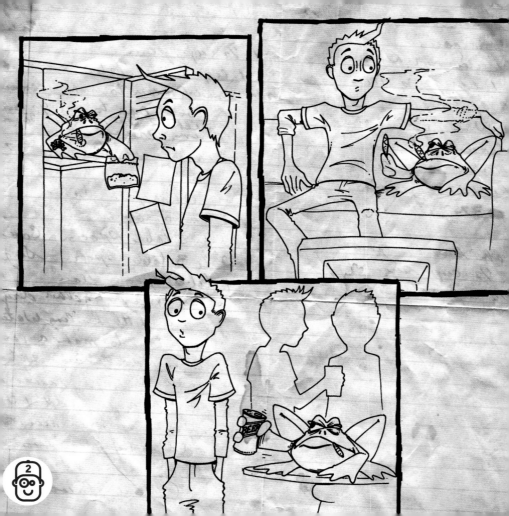

buzz

By Marcus Brotherton
MULTNOMAH PUBLISHERS® *SISTERS, OREGON*

FLIPSWITCH WARNING

FS This book may contain thought-provoking content you probably didn't hear in Sunday school. It should be discussed and debated with family and friends. This book does not contain the answers to all your questions, but helps you ask the right questions. Some biblical material may be inappropriate and shocking for people who want to be comfortable.